BUILD

UNIVERS

Pamela Fowler

Pamela Fowler

Illustrations by Rose Phillips

L I M E R I C K
T A L E S

europe books

www.europebooks.co.uk | info@europebooks.co.uk

ISBN 9791256971701
First edition: September 2025

Edited by Veronica Parise

LIMERICK

TALES

Big thank you to my two nieces,
Emma and Rosie,
my adopted nephew Adam,
my grandson Ian and amazing Kath at Long Eaton
library for helping this ageing technological dinosaur.

1.

Behold! A gay dragon am I
Those who mock me will
surely fry
I'm fierce, proud and bold
And cute, I've been told
If pink scales are your thing
I'm your guy.

Abercrombie the zombie is dead
From the bodies of others he'd fed
He had been unable
To keep his flesh stable
And in panic from him people fled.

Because he'd felt shame when he fed
Dark thoughts to his suicide led
This sensitive zombie
Our sad Abercrombie
Forgot he was already dead.

Mighty Tarzan is beating his chest

He's objecting to wearing a vest.
When he swings through the trees
With a Northerly breeze
It will pay to be cosily dressed.

The circus crowd started to boo
The quality acts were so few
But when Coco the clown
Felt his pants falling down
They applauded and clapped at the view.

2.

I climbed to the mouth of the cave
To enter it I must be brave
For the tales we are told
Cause the blood to run cold
As a demon seeks all to enslave.

There's the demon – it looks quite annoyed
This encounter I'd hoped to avoid
I showed it my bum
The sight struck it dumb
And it threw itself into a void.
(Job done)

I've met a dire sheep who's a bully
She glares at me fearsome and woolly.
If she starts to attack
There'll be no going back
And I'll land on my face in a gully.

My sister had more than her share
My jealousy brightly did flare

“You're the sister from hell”
Was her very loud yell
When she realised I'd cut off her hair.

Oh why do I choose the wrong queue?
I'd change this if only I knew
I could go berserk
And kill each slow jerk
But there's always another, or two.

3.

Cheeky teenager had smelly wind
He ate too many beans that were tinned.
They're one of the five
On which we all thrive
"And I find it amusing" he grinned.

Why did I have to be small?
I envy folk who are tall.
They can reach all top shelves
Way above us small elves
And don't blow away in a squall.

At my terror of spiders you jeer
I believe that you think it is queer
They move at great speed
And eye me with greed
I know that they can sense my fear.
(A spider dropped on me while I typed this -
Ugh! True.)

After a freak-out ....

Here am I, a rare troglodite
Though ugly I'm merry and bright
I sing out of tune
And laugh like a loon
But beware of my venomous bite.

This recipe's very complex
With butter, or maybe it's Trex?
My cooking is dire
The oven's on fire
I'd rather encounter T.Rex.

4.

Though book-keeping's all about credit
Our morale is badly in debit
The work is so boring
We hear the boss snoring
So let's blow the place up and then leg it.

With water I have a strong bond
Of swimming I am very fond
I splash and I spill
And flood with good will
And twice I fell into a pond.
(Not the same one)

I'm new to this computer game
But it seemed to be pretty tame
I typed like a good-un
Who said I'm a dud-un?
Then it all disappeared – what a pain.
(Okay then smartypants, what did I do?)

The alien invasion is here
We've got them all hooked on our beer
They love our fast cars
Get drunk in our bars
So let's shoot them while we're in the clear.

On a night filled with wonder and awe
Like a dream drawn from ancient folklore
On vast wings filled with light
A horse flew through the night
Could it be Pegasus that they saw?

5.

The man they all called boring Dwayne
Found thinking a terrible strain.
He never stopped talking
Not even when walking
So they shoved him under a train.

Boring Dwayne has turned up again
The train driver halted the train
Dwayne is back from the track
And his talking is back
So they stuffed him into a drain.

Smelly Dwayne has returned from the drain
And his talking is non-stop again
They had tried a big gag
Put his head in a bag
Then they gave up and fled to stay sane.

You can't kill a ghost with a gun
To try this will not be much fun

But what can you do
when you have no clue?
Maybe toss it a bun and then run?

Now here is a story macabre
You guessed, at the end there's a barb
From out of a mirror
There oozed a foul horror
If you get indigestion you could try bicarb.

6.

The Knight had to slay a fierce dragon
(Not the pink one)
They plied him with many a flagon
They said “Ride, bravely ride”
With a muttered aside
“If he lives he should go on the wagon”.

He fought very hard to survive
His sword into it he did drive
He was burnt to a crisp
Leaving him with a lisp
But the beautiful girl was alive.

She thanked him with many a kiss
And what followed on was sheer bliss
He'd slain the foul beast
They held a great feast
And he married his beautiful miss.
(How sweet. Yuk!)

This woman can lift up a car
She's famous in every low bar
She's been known to fight bears
Has a parrot that swears

And drinks whisky out of a jar.

Milkman Dan was a dreadful flirt
He couldn't resist a maid pert
The milkmaid did shudder
Then pulled on an udder
And milk in his eye she did squirt.

Though freedom is what I have sought
With misery my life is fraught
Because Alice my wife
Is the bane of my life
And each time I've run I've been caught.

7.

The Devil has had a bad day
He's looking for someone to flay
If you're in his sight
How tragic your plight
No way will you “Have a nice day”.

Cordelia the hippo's a wuss
Although she's as big as a bus
She's allergic to mud
When the river's in flood
She panics and makes a big fuss.

Though my landlady's daughter seemed weird
At my forebodings everyone jeered
When I died in my bed
From the food she had fed
My instincts proved right, as I'd feared.

While in spirit form I did remain
As my fluids she poured down the drain

Her new sausage machine
Had been shiny and clean
Now my blood had created a stain.

Her sausages made people sick
The coppers were told at the nick
My chronic disease
Uncovered her sleaze
And the case was then closed double quick.
(She now works in the prison kitchen)

8.

The success of the crime was inspired
The planning was all we desired
We'd stolen the gold
And lo and behold
With the proceeds I have now retired.
(Who said crime doesn't pay?
- er, “hello Detectives”)

Rapunzel let down her long hair
She did it because of a dare
She spread out her net
But who could she get?
As long as he's rich she won't care.

It is very hard work in the garden
Though my muscles have started to harden
I hate all slugs and snails
Leaving silvery trails
But it gets me away from the warden.

The murder solution was slow
The psychic put on a slick show
He consulted a bird
Which was madly absurd
When it pooped on his shoe - end of show.

Who would a bigamist be?
My husbands now total three
I created this mess
Which is causing me stress
Now a fourth wants to marry me.

9.

This fairy is Flowerdew
Magical potions she'd brew
Her boyfriend's a cheat
She gave him a sweet
Now all he can utter is "mew"

When mischievous sprite Flowerdew
Changed all the pink blossoms to blue
Colour blindness her plea
Though they let her off free
Her actions have banned her from Kew.

A pesky young man on a scooter
Would never stop sounding his hooter
If he doesn't desist
We will have to enlist
The aid of a lethal sharp shooter.

The con man is called Dead Eyed Dick
In prison he's learned a new trick
Going straight is in doubt
He can't wait to get out
And look for fat pockets to pick.

There's a piece missing out of his life
He's considering taking a wife
Better off with a dog
Keeps you fit when you jog
And avoids future marital strife.

There was a big guy who was hairy
Even spiders thought he was scary
He had a big belly
And was really smelly
But his wings were the clue – he's a fairy.

10.

The gnome wears a
jaunty red hat
He's jolly, so
round and so fat
He looks very cool
Sat next to my pool
But he's fat 'cos he just
ate my cat.

It's cold when you get to be old
In my youth I was always bold
But I know I can die
In the blink of an eye
Leaving all of my stories untold.
(Life's a beach).

Their arrival was from outer space
Seeming cultured and kind, this strange race
But they craved human flesh
Loving most when it's fresh
Before dining they pause to say grace.

Meet Rambo the vampire flea
He's hopping high now he's free
From a circus he'd fled
Where he hadn't been fed
Now blood he is seeking with glee.

His freedom is short-lived, you see
For while on his blood sucking spree
He's caught on the hop
And killed by a cop
This is Rambo's obituary.

11.

If you fart in a lift people glare
If it's smelly it causes a stir
If you fart in a crown
And it is mega loud
You could whistle to show you don't care.

On a mountain high
in the snow
The yetis live secret
and slow
With very large feet
Their footprints aren’t neat
And they puzzle the people below.

There was a big scary gorilla
Most people thought he was Godzilla
He lived in a tent
Because he owed rent
And there wasn't much work for a killer.

It seemed to have only one eye
He'd seen it appear in the sky
It had viewed his dark deed
Motivated by greed
And he watched as it started to cry.

It was just an old army jeep
Abandoned to ruse in a heap
With an aura so sad
Caused by traumas so bad
It has blood and death memories to keep.

12.

Not all dragons credit their brood
The masked one's a bully and crude
He has every bad trait
They despair of his fate
He's called Red and
he's in a bad mood.
(Watch out for the bold knight, Red).

There was an intelligent Yeti
With rivals both jealous and petty
On a day by the sea
If he planned carefully
He could push them all off the jetty.

We humans are all about sharing
And all need some loving and caring
If you don't like this rhyme
I have wasted my time
And my life will be just beyond bearing.
(Emotional blackmail wins – I hope)

Have you heard of this laughing loon
Who finds humour a happy boon?
If you've had a bad blow
Leaving you feeling low
It will soon cheer you up with a tune.

Nobody loves me, nobody cares
The old man ponders, sitting upstairs
They'll find when I'm dead
And my will is read
That the funds will all go to help bears.

13.

This is about a dead parrot
Starving and cold in a garret
He died for his art
But who gives a fart?
All he could paint was a carrot.

The thief thought that he was so smart, he
could steal all her bling at the party
His reactions were slow
Because he did not know
His victim was skilled at karate.

About vampires she is such a nut
Gives them blood, though she's no way a slut
They say “Fangs very much
We'll be keeping in touch”
Then they swagger away with a strut.
(Yeah yeah, not very punny).

The old house is haunted I hear
It's horribly worse than I fear
The ghosts of the dead
Fill me with great dread

So I hurry back home for more beer.

It didn't look like a toadstool
So I ate it. I was a fool
But it wasn't too tragic
It proved to be magic
Now my wings and my tail are so cool.

14.

I am a mermaid, your eyes are not wrong
Here in the ocean is where I belong
I practice a scale
While flicking my tail
Luring ships onto rocks with my song.

Success is no longer abundant
Technology's made me redundant
Radar is a curse
If it gets much worse
No singing to leave my descendant.

The girl with red hair was so naughty
She grew worse when her age reached forty
One fine night after dark
She ran wild in the park
And the nightie she wore was a shortie

Alone after dark late one night
A girl had a terrible fright
A soft sound on the stair
Gentle touch on her hair
Caused her quickly to turn on the light.

On seeing that no-one was there
The mirror she turned to to stare
The stairs always creaked
That's not why she shrieked
'twas the spider that crawled through her hair.

15.

Making gold is the alchemist's aim
Blending chemicals over a flame
If he meets with success
It will cause a world mess
As economies go down the drain.

A smart and intelligent llama
So handsome and gay, such a charmer
Had worked night and day
With no time to play
Creating a lewd diorama.

On a high branch is perched a tree frog
On his smartphone he's reading a blog.
He's sought on eBay
For someone who'll pay
For the rubbish he's trying to flog.
(the bat droppings were quite cheap)

The severed hand crawls 'cross the floor
It skitters right up to the door
From the wrist the blood leaks
Scaring all of the geeks

But the rest of the story's a bore.

I'm old and my knees have gone wonky
Such burdens they put on a donkey
With a multi-weight pack
And fat git on my back
My next incarnation's a monkey.

Such freedom I'll find as a monkey
No burdens to bear like a donkey
I'll climb with great ease
And pee from the trees
The females will all think I'm funky.

16.

In my dream the world’s end is nigh
Will it end with a bang, or sigh?
My nightmare is so drear
My alarm then I hear
“Armageddon up now” is my cry.

When the Grim Reaper says it's your time
You should try not to think it's a crime
The man with the sickle
Is not being fickle
It's his job - though that doesn't quite rhyme.

Behold the Pink Dragon! That's me
While off on a gay jamboree
Some villains I've caught
And battles I've fought
And now for a nice cup of tea.

Naughty Bessie's tail started to wag
As she sniffed in the
fisherman's bag
With a fish on his line
Bessie wasted no time
As a sandwich she stole from his bag

Old Bony Maloney's a phony
He tripped on a path that was stony
He claimed compensation
Bankrupted the Nation
But he'd slipped on his spilt macaroni.

Reading crystal balls seemed very quirky
When I tried to look in all was murky
Then the sun on it bright
Caused a fire to ignite
And the fire crew tried not to look smirky.

17.

His friends very loudly did mock
At savings he kept in a sock
When the banks all go bust
His precautions prove just
Then to him for a loan they all flock.

They set up a large institution
An environmental solution
It worked very well
Though how could they tell
The extractor fan caused vast pollution.

There was an odd person named Stella
Who stabbed victims with her umbrella
When they started to smell
And the flies gave her hell
She buried them deep in her cellar.

The posh lady looked very swanky
Inside she was feeling quite cranky
It is never much fun
When your nose starts to run
And you come out forgetting a hanky.

The snake hunter's looking for glory
Though worried that snake bites
are gory
With coils round him tight
His future's not bright
Not poisoned but squashed
ends his story.

18.

He appeared to be love's young dream
But things never are what they seem
She caught him one night
And now he's in flight
If she finds him he'll gain a high scream.

My sculptor friend's fame quickly grew
For her statues there is quite a queue
When she answers her 'phone
We all give a loud groan
For she answers each time with "Statue".

Jack's unable to buy a new car
As his cash flow is well below par
He builds a car kit
Q registers it
Now he's noticed by all near and far.

In his role as detective he swore
At the crime scene he viewed
from the door
A good living was made
From the parts actors played

Of dead bodies all covered with gore.

But no-one jumped up at the end
This massacre wasn't pretend
A real 'tec. took over
And tried to discover
If the series was due to extend.

He worked with a money scam crew
His wealth it just grew and it grew
He had gone to great pains
To hide ill-gotten gains
But the cops and the tax men all knew.
(Gotcha!)

19.

When I opened my gate coming home
For the wreckage I saw you'll atone
A quick chant at Stonehenge
Aimed to get my revenge
For the damage you've done to my gnome.
(Okay, so he ate your cat too?)

The tarot card warning was clear
"Remember these words" said the seer
"Beware of the snake
Your life it will take"
But he thinks he has nothing to fear.

He wakes in his bed with a start
Aware of his fast-pounding heart
He feels the snake's bite
The warning was right
From his life he will sadly depart.

It's her first space
travelling trip
But deep in her
menopause grip
She's hot in the face
And asks for more space
So they throw her out of the ship

A fisherman caught a gold fish
If freed it would grant him a wish
It puzzled him so
He just didn't know
So he wished that he knew what to wish.

20.

If the Grim Reaper says it's
your time
You should pray you've
committed no crime
If you go on the run
It will not be much fun
When you're thrown in some very hot slime.

The spaceship sent down a bright beam
It took up a whole rugby team
With their after-game pongs
And their crude rugby songs
It was fun to hear aliens scream.

We live in a very old house
At drawbacks we try not to grouse
A loud bump in the night
It's the naughty house sprite
And we know we've a resident mouse.

When I ask him “What star sign are you?”
He refuses to give me a clue
His top half is male

Horse body and tail
Then he laughs as he gallops from view.

I doubt that you've heard of our Joe
Here's something that you might not know
He tamed a baboon
Taught it how to croon
I'm entitled to crow, Joe's my bro.

21.

Pink Dragon returns to say “Hi”
I know you've all missed me.
Don't cry
I've been on a quest
And had a good rest
Your hero is back – here am I.

Pursuing some top gangland primes
I've been through some very hard times
Lured them into a trap
With a 'Pow’ and a 'Zap'
Thus ending their multiple crimes.

She'd studied the runes a long time
Although friends thought it was a crime
Then a ghost Viking chief
Warned she could come to grief
Because some of the runes aren't benign.

He had fashioned a golem from clay
As a guard for his journey next day
But it rained in the night
Such a pitiful sight

As the golem just melted away.

The funeral of the comic was due
And the mourners had filled every pew
He was known for his pranks
For his jokes they gave thanks
Then the body leapt up and yelled “Boo”.

A Griffin's a vision of glory
It features in legends most hoary
It guards a great treasure
With worth beyond measure
A robber's fate would be most gory.

22.

The locals gave it the name Mabel
The gargoyle that sat on a gable
When one night it flew down
Terrorising the town
They all cowered under a table.
(It didn't like the name Mabel. Preferred Clark).

All Orcs seem to have a bad name
But only a few are to blame
My pet name is Toot
I'm really quite cute
I'll send you a picture to frame.

The hero did not feel despair
As captors locked him in their lair
For with one mighty bound
And a loud booming sound
He broke free and took to the air.

On a hill she parked her golf trolley

Forgetting the brake was her folly
It ran down to the lake
With her fast in its wake
Mighty splash went the golfer and trolley.

The cowboy had found a dark lair
He thought he could hide out in there
But he had a close shave
With an Indian brave
And that's why he now has no hair.

23.

The hand reader told her a tale
Her hollow palms showed she could fail
But her curving heart line
Shows her loving is fine
But she's hoped for a dark handsome male.

My favourite tree is a yew
In a churchyard so old it grew
It has roots way down deep
Where the old coffins sleep
And all of their secrets it knew.

Every night in the snow and the rain
Poor old Moggy is kicked out again
He would rather be snug
By the fire on a rug
He is house trained, why can't he remain?

The insect who called himself Styx
Had failed to attract the stick chicks
He had posed like a star
But was judged below par
He needed to learn some new tricks.

The crocodile's stage name is Jaws
His acting wins him great applause
When he's not on the stage
He is kept in a cage
And his contract has no 'get out' clause.

24.

Fat Bluey the fly never tired
Of polluting food, he's inspired
But with great elan
I squirted my can
And with legs in the air he expired.

The creature that lives in Loch Ness
Is suffering from serious stress
Each time it swims out
To hunt a large trout
Reporters all swarm from the press.

It’s enough to make angels weep
Old Dobbin has died in his sleep
Now each day he can play
In a meadow of hay
Rewards for his labours he'll reap.

It is one of the old sailor's tales
His belief in its truth never fails

The souls of the drowned
Are still all around
He has seen their pale form in some gales.

On a mountain high on a peak
A climber encountered a freak
He'd tried not to stare
As it was quite bare
Though it had a posh voice for a freak.

25.

Pink Dragon was out on the prowl
He thought that he'd heard something growl
He disturbed a mad skunk
In a great pile of junk
The scent that it squirted smelled foul.

The smell around him seemed to flow
To clean it was proving too slow
To get rid of the stink
He dived into the drink
And found a sea dragon below.

Blue Dragon had swum a long way
To seek for a good place to stay
On his lonely quest
He'd never have guessed
That a new friend would brighten his day.

Police held a modern convention
To focus on new crime prevention
There were coppers in drag
A converted old lad
But old staff can't wait for their pension.

I saw an old man looking sad
And wondered what could be so bad
I felt pity for him
He was looking so grim
Then I realised that he was my Dad.
(Needed a hug)

26.

Blue Dragon was hunting the deep
For Neptune, who had been asleep
when his trident was nicked
And Blue Dragon was picked
To hunt down the opportune thief.
(Hired a sniffer dogfish)

When the sniffer fish followed the trail
Neptune's trident was found in a whale
A good cloud on the snout
Made the trident shoot out
Now the whale is applying for bail.

A ghost haunts the old castle keep
Its sobbing disturbing their sleep
Why does it remain?
What's causing its shame?
What you sow you must surely reap.

All take heed before tempted to slay
On your death as a ghost you will stay
In a temper so wild

He had murdered his child
And this penalty now he must pay.

When you age all parts firm start to sag
A young woman becomes an old hag
What was lovely before
Is attractive no more
She now looks like an old man in drag.

27.

I've visited so many stores
The right tool to find for my cause
If your spade is quite nice
And you quote a fair price
The next grave I dig won't be yours.

A young man who was rather small
Was desperate to grow very tall
In a grow-bag he stood
But it wasn't much good
He grew very large feet but that's all.

With guns decimating their prey
The hunters continued to slay
I remember the day
When the birds flew away
And the sky was left empty and grey.

How about a leap in the dark?
It's a challenge, just for a lark

It's a mystery dare
Meant to see if you scare
To test your adventurous spark.

You could risk too much if you knew
What danger might come after you
So stay in your bed
And cover your head
Or better yet, hide in the loo.

28.

I was walking one day and felt weary
Came across a strange pub that looked eerie
When I looked the next day
It had vanished away
An illusion? That could be one theory.

A friend said that he'd test this theory
His interest was anything eerie
He was writing a book
For the pub he would look
Both are gone and I've searched 'til I'm weary.

In the jungle a deep steady beat
It's the pounding of multiple feet
In a pot on the fire
He's about to expire
All because they ran out of fresh meat.

I'm Tootie the Orc here again
To be a great star is my aim
My picture looks well
I really can tell
You've chosen a beautiful frame.

The singer is a very fine tenor
Has unlikely red hair, dyed with henna
I played cards for his disc
Took a very big risk
But I'll sell it to you for a tenner.

29.

An incredible shrinking baboon
Is beseeching a witch for a boon
He is under a curse
If it doesn't disperse
He will vanish away very soon.

In my fish bowl I have a fine castle
My bad memory earns me much hassle
I'm a goldfish at play
Bad memory? No way
Swimming round I see castle. What castle?

They all viewed what washed up with the tide
In a bottle a message was spied
The date was quite new
From a shipwrecked crew
Who were found when the search went worldwide.

Do not enter the vampire bus
This action would prove perilous
If the door opens wide

And it sucks you inside
Your end would be most atrocious.

How to balance the ship was a riddle
In the band a big man played the fiddle
As his girth was so wide
The ship dipped to one side
They yelled “Quickly, get into the middle”.

30.

There was no face within the deep cowl
A ghost monk on its dark nightly prowl
Through the ruins it crept
It seemed that it wept
Then was gone with a low mournful howl.

In a closet so dark and so deep
Mr Bones was disturbing her sleep
He rattled his bones
Gave heart-rending groans
For her secrets were heavy to keep.
(For Rachel. Sorry I dropped him out of the window).

A kidnapper took Mr Bones
To find out the secrets he owns
No nails and no ears
No eyes, so no tears
No torture would work, he's just bones.

Each day when I walk down the stairs
I check that there's only eight pairs
At the bottom one day

More stairs led me away
Where they led to still gives me nightmares.

Jolly Roger's a pirate so bold
He has jewels and chests full of gold
He buried them deep
But after a sleep
He forgot where he put them, I'm told.

31.

I've a distant cousin named Rory
Who told me an interesting story
Found a Cyclops eye
In a shepherd’s pie
He's a terrible liar, our Rory.

On wings that are trailing bright flame
A phoenix has risen again

A glorious sight
Of power and might

From ashes a new life to claim.

He's Elvis, the crooning baboon
Joe's taught him a catchy new tune
He now plays his guitar
In a trendy new bar
And his next disc is coming out soon.

The lovely young girl has red eyes
It happens each time that she cries
This red-eyed Banshee
Will howl mournfully
And won't stop until somebody dies.

The kids loved their toy Ducky Quack
Her feathers were light brown and black
Her bright yellow beak
When given a tweak
Emitted a very loud quack.

32.

He'd thought that he'd heard someone squealing
The sight he then viewed was appealing
She'd reduced what she ate
And had lost so much weight
That she found herself stuck to the ceiling.

The leader of one rival gang
Had threatened that we would all hang
When he pulled out a gun
I had thought we were done
'til down dropped a flag that said “Bang”.

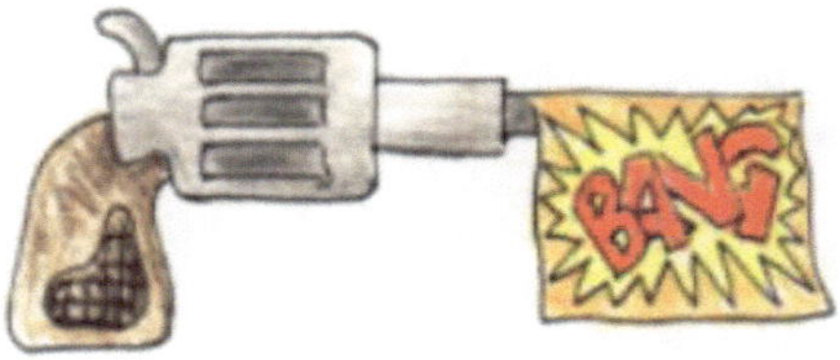

I've recently met Neptune's daughter
She has a pink trident he'd bought her
Its mystical power
Makes enemies cower
To be wary of whales Neptune taught her.

His seduction with falseness did ooze
So she thumped him, it left a large bruise
She'd heard it before
It was such a bore
Now she's off on a well-deserved cruise.

I was cleaning the kitchen one day
And was putting the toaster away
I picked up a large crumb
It moved under my thumb
A loud screech as I threw it away.

33.

To escape on a ship was her plan
But she's found by her father's law man
“You're too late” she cried
Then leapt over the side
And into the arms of her merman.

Pink Dragon had formed a new plan
With typical flair and elan
The Pink and the Blue
A crime scene to view
To help the police where they can.

Police crime-busting dragons are we
We're a new detective agency
With fire and with claw
We'll fight for the law
In the air, on the land, in the sea.
Got the badges.

Though a crypt is so spooky at night
It's the place where he hides from the light
He murdered and slew
Not leaving a clue

But the dragons will soon end his blight.

He thought that he'd found Merlin's cave
With crystals to sell and to save
But what he did not know
Was when they start to glow
His end would be an early grave.

34.

“I remember the war...” they all groan
And he suddenly finds he's alone
Now the young ones don't care
It's a sorry affair
But they all help him work his smartphone.

The elf has such very large ears
He hears all the whispers and sneers
Only he hears the sound
Of the opening ground
Then everyone else disappears.

He thought to try past life regression
This had been a long-time ambition
He discovered he'd killed
So much blood he had spilled
He's a century late for confession.

It was known that the tunnel was haunted
But the drunken man hadn't been daunted
He was found the next day

All his blood sucked away
No-one dares now, not even when taunted.

Rochaw was the sewer rat king
Wherever he went fear he'd bring
The old snake did not fear
And the rat's end was near
One gulp saw the end of the king.

35.

Once we went on a drunken spree
Just my old friend Stinky and me
We got lost in a fog
And attacked by a dog
No dog, now two werewolves are we.

The girl on the flying trapeze
Soars high to disguise knobbly knees

There's a hole in her tights
She is quite scared of heights

And the monkeys have given her fleas.

Who is that wearing a mask?
"What is the mystery?", you ask
He's very like Zorro
What happens tomorrow
When everyone takes off their mask?

Only I and one other know
The masked man who looked like Zorro
It's a secret so deep
One I promised to keep
If told it will be to my sorrow,

To track Zorro the trail has gone cold
It's too risky for even the bold
The last man who tried
Mysteriously died
There are facts not allowed to unfold.
A good guess might be a mole.

36.

My parents have both passed away
I look at their picture each day
Then another appeared
In the picture, so weird
It's an aunt who had died that same day.

I looked at the picture today
Another had joined the array
My own face appeared
It's something I'd feared
I'm with family now, it's okay.

To be called sparrow legs wasn't fun
For a tall girl, though fast she could run
But her triumph was sweet
On thin legs and fast feet
An Olympic Gold Medal she'd won.

The girls named the ghost Natty Belle
She treated the sisters quite well
But gave brave men nightmares

Their own Dad feared the stairs
He claimed he'd been pushed when he fell.

The doll with red eyes makes flesh creep
It wanders about while they sleep
So they chop off its head
Double-check it is dead
Then make sure that they bury it deep.

37.

The vintage dress was a good fit
She loved flouncing round wearing it
A woman named Bess
Still haunted the dress
With two women inside, a tight fit.

A man had a serious twitch
Frustrating him to a high pitch
He drove down a lane
In the pouring rain
And his twitch sent his car in a ditch.

We anthropomorphise creatures
To give them appealing features
At the end of the day
A key role they all play
But there's little to love about leeches.

They thought it would be such fun
To enter the latest fun run

They ran in a row
So no-one would know
Who led, so then everyone won.

He's well known as a trouble-shooter
Quite mobile on his trusty scooter
A problem to solve?
It is his resolve
To thump all your foes on the hooter.

38.

When you're young there's so much time to play
You don't think about old age today
There's plenty of time
You're still in your prime
But the years just keep drifting away.

It was such an enormous nest

So huge, it was surely a jest

A large head popped out
It had a long snout

The elephant bird proved a pest.

The beautiful girl was named Jean
So gorgeous at just seventeen
Through a time warp she fell
It worked out rather well
In an alien world she's now queen.

The magician had learned a new trick
He had practised until it was slick
When the girl fell apart
It had broken his heart
And he ended up locked in the nick.

The taste of her food was divine
The pain in his gut the first sign
They tested her stew
But that gave no clue
The poison had been in the wine.

39.

I'm Tootie the Orc of great fame
I have now accomplished my aim
With the help of my club
And free rounds in the pub
I'm met every day with acclaim.

Kanga is a cranky old Roo

She's lived far too long in their view

She's nobody's pet
Has bitten the vet.

And given them hell at the zoo.

Red Dragon is looking for trouble
And buildings to burn down to rubble
There's danger ahead
When dealing with Red
Prepare to defend at the double.

Incy spider's web weaving's not fine
All his threads do not seem to align
He'd checked on the Net
For help he might get
But his web is not what they design.

She really thought it was a joke
A frog on her bed when she woke
A prince when she kissed
How could she resist?
Now she has a most musical croak.

40.

I am tiring of making new rhymes
About villains committing dark crimes
I'll call it a day
Go out for a play
And return when the dinner bell chimes.

Now I've been out and had a good play
And enjoyed a fine meal on a tray
I'll find a new rhyme
It may take some time
Then go on until I'm old and grey.
Oh dear, I forgot I already am.

When the Grim Reaper comes for you
You may have to wait in a queue
If you stand at the end
He may pick on your friend
But you'll never escape from his view.

It is time for her final goodbye
She's enjoyed knowing you, it's no lie
She's had so much fun
But now it is done
She'll miss you and try not to cry.
(Does)

The home team's goal kick caused a roar
And supporters chanted for more
At the top of their game
With bright visions of fame
And pride in the colours they wore.

41.

Your Pink Dragon's returned from the grave

Where I fought the undead in their cave

I burned out their lair

Not leaving a hair

Roaring back with a smile and a wave.

The old man considered his life
Now free from all marital strife
He looked back at the day
When his wife ran away
And ruined another man's life.

The chocolate addict's a gnat
On sugar it grew very fat
A chocolate flake
Was too much to take
And it burst with a very loud splat.

An earwig said to his love bug
“You're ugly but give me a hug”
“That's not very kind,
I have a good mind
To slap you across your smug mug”.

At an Old Men in Drag convention
The rivalry's causing some tension
The prize for best wig
Was a little fat pig
And a bright red toupee got a mention.

42.

Broody hens on MacDonald's farm
Stole his laptop, meaning no harm
With a click click here
And a click click there
They broke it, to Mac's great alarm.

Though Grasshopper worked hard for his master
His levitation was a disaster
He'd hovered quite well
Lost focus and fell
And he ended the lesson in plaster.

The panel consists of three mice
Their answers are quick and precise

Questions about cheese

Are answered with ease

But caught cheating they all
pay the price.

(Cut off their tails with a carving knife).

I was lying down resting my back
In the ceiling I noticed a crack
A red eye looked down
at me with a frown
So I leapt up and started to pack.

A thief had been caught, same old lag
What gave him away? What's the snag?
The stripes on his socks
and shirt, the pick-locks
Or the sack on his back that said SWAG?

43.

A creature that lived in a bog
Was wishing that it had a dog
It would be so good
To play in the mud
With a friend like a dog in a bog.

Yes, the elephant bird proved a pest

Doesn't listen when we all protest

Plays rock on his trunk
His nest's full of junk

We all flee to the hills
for a rest.

For a lifetime of crime comes the day
The full price of each dark deed to pay
The judgement is fair
And no-one will care
When the black cloud has sucked them away.

There once was a paranoid bear
Who feared she was losing her hair
When she stole a blond wig
Though it was rather big
She loved flaunting her long golden hair.

A golf ball flew high in the air
The golfer watched it with great care
Then a bird flying high
Took it out of the sky
While all watched it with open-mouthed stare.

44.

The puffed-up king toad was bombastic
His tongue was so sharp and sarcastic
But he loses his crown
As he jumps up and down
When they dangle down bait on elastic.

In a library a bookworm roams free

It is gnawing on books with great glee

The librarians' quest
Is to banish the pest

When they squashed it they
all yelled "Yippee".

A poor man is suffering from man flu.
He thinks that his death must now be due
He snifflers and moans
With heart-rending groans
While his wife longs to poison his stew.

At a fairground a lady named Jane
Took a ride on a spooky ghost train
When it vanished in smoke
All thought it a joke
But her friends never saw her again.

A newt and a frog were at war
An undying feud they both swore
When a carp muscled in
They joined forces to win
Getting rid of the carp mattered more.

45.

When the vicar was seeking a clue
He was looking beneath every pew
Found his missing new vest
Was a cosy mouse nest
And the church cleaning lady said “Eww”.

A laughing hyena was he
His pack mates were howling with glee
He won't live it down
He feels such a clown
The joke is he's stuck up a tree.

Red Dragon is guarding his hoard

Where ill-gotten gains he
has stored

A fool-hardy thief

Would soon come to grief

That he's lethal should not be ignored.

The Grim Reaper is here once again
Every time he appears it's a pain
When he peers from his hood
He is up to no good
And your hopes for long life are in vain.

A grave digger dug up an egg
The hatchling had only one leg
She hops at great speed
He can't guess her breed
He adopts her and calls her his Peg.

46.

The old crow hears the wailing and woe
Sees the slaughter take place down below
Now each night the man hears
Though he blocks up his ears
"I am only a crow, but I know"

It was dark, though the moonlight was bright
As they walked through the graveyard that night
From out of a grave
An arm gave a wave
A speed record they broke in their flight.

I'm Tootie the Orc of great fame
A new star now carries my name

I've bashed many a head
And bribery has led

To the King dubbing me a Dame.

A young Dactyl was nick-named Terra
But time proved this had been an error
It dislikes flying high
And when darkness is nigh
It shakes under its blankets in terror.

A monkey is trying to fly
Flaps his arms and jumps from on high
For a job he has seen
In a flight magazine
Is only for those who can fly.

47.

The aliens went home, they gave in
They really believed they could win

We're too stubborn to beat
They admitted defeat

But they've robbed us of all
of our gin.

Some facts of this mystery are gone
But a few stories linger on

Everything left in place
Of the aliens, no trace

But some gin-making families were gone.

When exploring a tomb underground
In a sealed room a demon was found
To undo its chain
A wish each would gain
They are wary, for why was it bound?

The men found it hard to resist
As each had a long bucket list
But they re-sealed the tomb
Left it to its doom
Though regretting the chances they've missed.

Little brother drives big sister spare
He'll try anything for a dare
He draws in her books
Her lipstick he sucks
Writes rude words on the wall up the stair,
(With very bad spelling)

48.

A stranger is in a strange land
He's lost in a vast sea of sand
No water in sight
And so cold at night
No soul round to give him a hand.

He's resigned to the fact he will die
It's so lonely, no soul passing by
Then Pink Dragon appears
And allays all his fears
On the dragon's back safely he'll fly.

On a misty morning in May
A bride wakes on her wedding day

Her groom at the church
Is left in the lurch

For an elf prince steals his
bride away.

He needed to test his invention
To access another dimension
But he'd failed to learn
The way to return
Disappearance was not his intention.

He was watching the new lambs at play
Celebrating the first day of May
Fell down in the gorse
Got bit by a horse
Now his favourite dinner is hay.

49.

She heard singing float over the lake
The singer was a large water snake
The snake's charm worked so well
She fell under its spell
And she drifted and drowned in the lake.

Roll up for the fun of the fair

To visit the side shows, and stare

At men wearing kilts

While dancing on stilts

Look up at the view if you dare.

What's the worst thing that makes your flesh creep?
What dread thought makes you cower and weep?
Is it dolls with red eyes?
Or gross maggots and flies?
Or what lurks 'neath your bed while you sleep?

Where did you go to my friend?
What did I do to offend?
We had so much fun
You brought out the sun
I never believed it would end.

And now you are back with a smile
Enchanting with charm and with style
What caused you to flee?
Will you always be
Avoiding my questions with guile?

50.

Here's a puzzle to solve if you care
What is brown and is covered with hair?
A tiger to be
When it has won free
Have you got it? It's a woolly bear.
(Tiger Moth caterpillar)

I felt sure I had heard of a snark
I believed it might live in a park
Looked it up on the 'net
Just how wrong could I get?
It appears I was way off the mark.
(Look it up for yourself)

The divers had found an old wreck

An octopus lurked on the deck

It held them at bay
Demanded they pay

So they fobbed it off with a dud cheque.

The hero lies dead on the stage
Destroyed by his rival's wild rage
It was not in the script
But his self-control slipped
It's the last time he'll exit a stage.

A moth round a flame loves to dance
The flame puts the moth in a trance
It lights up her wings
Her little heart sings
She risks all for the joy of the dance.

51.

When Elvis, Joe's crooning baboon
Had started to sing out of tune
Said a girl broke his heart
Means to make a new start
Writing love songs to sing to the moon.

This green lizard is known as Echo
He's agile and fast, is this gecko
But he's falling about
And his balance is out
Best guess? He's been at the Prosecco.

Her cat-eating gnome's on the run
He's hunted by all with a gun
He's on every hit list
The last sniper just missed
They'd failed tempting him with a bun.
(A cat might have worked. Sorry)

There's a pointy-eared man nick-named Spock
Who's so poor all his things are in hock
When he foiled a bank raid
With insurance they paid
He went straight out and bought a big clock.

For me watching cricket's a bore
Although I like knowing the score
But I had to admit
That I perked up a bit
When our local team won with a four.

52.

While carrying a baby a stork
Had observed he was stalked
by a hawk
With care placed his load
On a quiet road
And said "Okay, I think we
should talk"

(Hawk)

"I think that you have the wrong child
And it's driving my poor mate wild
Check the baby for wings
And such relevant things"
So they checked and it was the hawk's child.

His hair was in need of a crop
So he sought for a barber's shop
But a demon pair
Had rented the chair
So his head not his hair got the chop.

The new cook was a lady from Crewe
With a recipe she could not do
She had tried to toast it
Had failed to roast it
So she flushed the whole lot down the loo.

The ghost hunter's had a bad day
The ghost wouldn't come out to play
After howling all night
And worn out causing fright
It had taken a ghost holiday.

53.

In an apple there lived a worm
It thought that its tenure was firm
Someone took a large bite
Caused the poor worm a fright
In the apple there's now half a worm.

Another young lady from Crewe
Discovers she's locked in the loo
When she causes a stink (pun not intended)
Those in line waiting think
“Serves her right for jumping the queue.

An old and most devious mole
In life he had only one goal

He'd cheat and he'd lie
Most tricks he would try

For the worms from his rivals he stole.

When I grow up a pixie I'll be
I will make a warm home in a tree
With no taxes to pay
Or commute every day
No more scary high bills – I'll be free.

A snail and a whale were best friends
Despite many negative trends
As each of them grey
Their bond was like glue
But a deep dive gave snail friend the bends.

54.

On a mountain covered in now
An eerie light started to glow
The people hear screams
They're plagued with bad dreams
And all feel such terror and woe.

A thick cloud began to descend
No psychic could predict the end
Some thought it too odd
Some prayed to their god
Then pranksters yelled out “It's pretend”.
(So they shot them).

The demon bus driver won't stop
She'd screamed very loud for a cop
She'd dinged on the bell
This tale won't end well
She'll be added to this killer's crop.

To show off in a punt is too rash
He believes he looks dishy and flash
With pole stuck in the mud
All the signs are not good
And he lands in the drink with a splash.

When a vampire's teeth ache it's bad luck
If his teeth are removed he'll be stuck
False teeth are too blunt
When on a blood hunt
He can't bite on a neck, only suck.

55.

A Kraken appears from the deep
Disturbing Blue Dragon's deep sleep
Its mission – to kill
And much blood to spill
Caring little that loved ones will weep.

As Blue Dragon is pledged to keep law
So the Kraken he greets with a roar
With a huge clash they meet
To the Kraken's defeat
It slinks back to the deep feeling sore.

A man I know makes limoncello
He is a most popular fellow
He has visits galore
They form queues at his door
And sleep on his floor feeling mellow.

A face peers through a rusty grill
The locals believe it's Old Bill
It is haggard and drawn
With a look so forlorn
If it upsets you, go take a pill.

One night a man dreams he is falling
The fear that he feels is appalling
He lands with a bump
On his head a large lump
And he wakes his wife up with loud bawling.

56.

A peacock spread out his bright tail
Put one of his feathers on sale
A girl with a hat
Said she would have that
It went to her head from his tail.

Peacock feathers have earned a bad name
And as crime was this young lady's game
With a plume in her hat
How could cops not miss that?
So she's nicked and the peacock's to blame.

A tomcat with large golden eyes
One morning had such a surprise

Saw a mouse in his house
He then pounced on the mouse

And the mouse had the greater surprise.

On Halloween night every year
A headless horseman will appear
A bad headache has led
him to take off his head
On this night when he drinks too much beer.

Why do sports commentators shout loud?
Do they think that it excites the crowd?
If it is a dull game
And they shout, it's still tame
Is a volume control not allowed?

57.

Searched the haunted house for a rough sleeper
Grew more sinister as we went deeper
As we looked through each room
Through the murk and the gloom
What a shock when we found the Grim Reaper.

When the golden haze began to part
He beheld a white horse with a cart
The horse said “Get in”
With such a sly grin
To obey might not be very smart.

But he climbed in the cart – what a prat
They took off at the drop of a hat
At the end of the track
There was no going back
It's the end of his tale and that's that.

The ship had a skeleton crew
Their bones were the obvious clue
It had been a long trip
With no food on the ship
And the Captain said he meant to sue.

Felt exciting to go wild swimming
With energy they were all brimming
From down deep something rose
And bit off all their toes
And that was the end of wild swimming.

58.

To make fireworks they had formed a gang
For safety they cared not a hang
But their sparkling plot
Turned out far too hot
They went out with a very loud bang.

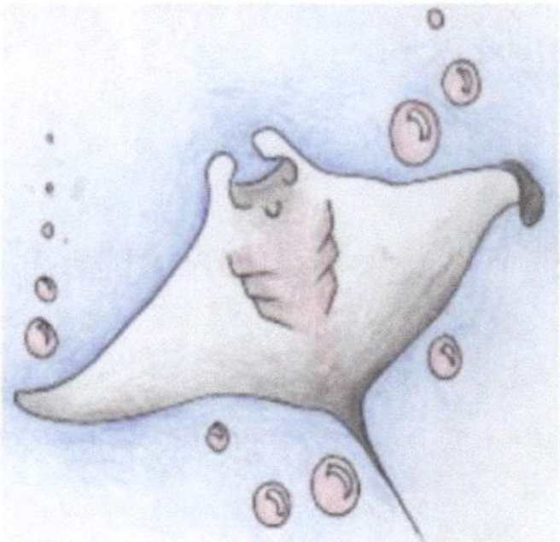

Ray was just swimming along
Humming a soft shanty song
He's an old manta ray
Who's enjoying the day
With a tail that is smooth and strong.

Very few in the deep think think he's prey
He's a large gentle giant old ray
He has jaws open wide
Sifting plankton inside
As he swims in the ocean each day.

Her gnome hides in a deep catacomb
Gangs of cats stopped him from going home
He is all scratched and beat
Has admitted defeat
Meet the new vegetarian gnome.
(Can go home now)

On days when you feel sad and low
Get out, take a bus and just go
Find a park or wood
By water is good
Breathe the air, hear the birds, and let go.

59.

A cave by a large waterfall
Held bones that when found caused a squall
A large mammoth tooth
Provided the truth
That the mammoth had died just last Fall.

Dark demons took over our world
In slavery we were all hurled

Who could help our plight
In this darkest night?

Would this be the end of
our world?

It wasn't the end of the game
Pink Dragon roared in with his flame
With his trusty crew
The Red and the Blue
They ended the demons' foul game.
(Yes, even Big Bad Red)

In a field when the sun was high
I laid down and looked at the sky
Watched a small bird in flight
Was enjoying the sight
When it dropped a splat right in my eye.

60.

On a farm lived a demented turkey
Its behaviour decidedly quirky
It would gobble and sway
Hold the postman at bay
So they turned it into turkey jerky.

The horrid child never stopped nagging
Its' parents' resistance was flagging
If now they give in
They will never win
And the only solution is gagging.

In a cave a knight found a sword
It called to him "Hey knight, I'm bored"
He must now make a choice
And disliking its voice
He throws it back onto the hoard.

But the magical sword was not done
It had waited too long for some fun
Before he could leave
It clung to his sleeve
So the knight shot the sword with his gun.

Grim Reaper will have the last word
To hope for escape is absurd
This immortal soul
Continues his role
Still reaping the last time I heard.

THE END

61.

Okay then:

Just one more.

From a very deep hole in the ground
Came a shape that looked like a large hound
It asked “Is it morn”
Then gave a vast yawn
And climbed back in the hole in the ground.

GOODNIGHT

europe books